Antonelli's River Inn

Antonelli's River Inn

by
Carlyn Luke Reding

graphics and photography by
Glynn Monroe Irby

Edited by
Susie Kelly Flatau

Old River Productions

Antonelli's River Inn
Copyright © 2003 by Carlyn Luke Reding.
All rights reserved.

First Edition

ACKNOWLEDGEMENTS

The author wishes to acknowledge prior publication of variations
of the following poems and interview which appear in this book.

"Afternoon of Gulls," **Anniversary DiVerseCity**, 2002, AIPF
"Antonelli's River Inn," **3 Savanna Blue**, 2000, Plain View Press
"From School to Other Times," **3 Savanna Blue**
"Leaf Dreams," **3 Savanna Blue**
"Points Further East," **Suddenly V**, 2003, Stone River Press
"Saturday Morning at *Sainte-Mere-Eglise*," **Feeding the Crow**, 1998, Plain View Press
"Sleeping Arrangements #41," **3 Savanna Blue**
"Sometimes on Valentine's Day," **Feeding the Crow**
"Strange Birds Sing," **3 Savanna Blue**
"The Dance of the Brown Pelicans," **3 Savanna Blue**
"The Heart in Time," **Feeding the Crow**
"The Tarpon Inn," **Feeding the Crow**
"Tugs and Barges," **3 Savanna Blue**
"Whitecaps and Ravens," **Feeding the Crow**
Interview with the Author, **Sol-Magazine**, 2001

Cover art by Doris Munson, a resident of Lake Jackson, Texas. She teaches art in the Brazosport area and enriches her talent by studying abroad. The native Texan chose Antonelli's River Inn as a subject because of its local color and charm, distinctive architecture, and quality root beer.

Reding, Carlyn Luke
Antonelli's River Inn

    p.   cm.   photos   graphics   interviews

1. Poet—Texas—Literary landmarks. 2. Historical places—Texas. 3. Antonelli, Henry. 4. Poets, American—20th century. 5. American poetry—Texas. 6. Texas—History, local. 7. Literary landmarks—American poetry—Texas.

I. Title. II. Author. III. Poetry. IV. Monograph.

ISBN: 0-9728868-0-X

TZZ 811.08R61   811.5R   2003091233

Old River Productions
3005 South Lamar Boulevard
Suite D-109-331
Austin, Texas 78704

Printed in the United States of America
by Morgan Printing, Austin, Texas

Antonelli's River Inn

Contents

Introduction   *x*
Editor's Note   *xiii*

SECTION 1: *In the Shade of Latticed Arches*

from Conversations with Two Rivers	2
Bone Dust	3
from Conversations with Two Rivers	4
With Each Swing of the Pendulum	5
Memory of Fog and Mist	6
Crossbars	7
jelli 1	8
Clock in the Clouds	9
from Conversations with Two Rivers	10
Time Honored	11
from Conversations with Two Rivers	12
Poetry Shards	13
jelli 2	14
The Heart in Time	15
Rocking Horse Finish	16
from Conversations with Two Rivers	20
Memorywalk	21
from Conversations with Two Rivers	22
A Celebration of the Feminine	23
Saturday Morning at *Sainte-Mere-Eglise*	24
Misappropriation of Oleanders	26
In the Shadow of Los Alamos	27
Underground Undertow	28
Wreath of Dolphins	29
from Conversations with Two Rivers	30
Camera Works	31
jelli 3	32
Back to the Beginning	33

SECTION 2: *Root Beer and Painted Rocks*

from Conversations with Two Rivers	36
First Coffee First Snow	37
from Conversations with Two Rivers	38

The Tarpon Inn	39
from Conversations with Two Rivers	40
Tugs and Barges	41
Sometimes on Valentine's Day	42
From School to Other Times	43
jelli 4	44
Plums to Pines	45
French Quarter Boutique	46
Points Further East	47
jelli 5	48
Acequias in Shadow	49
jelli 6	50
Leaving Los Alamos	51
Sleeping Arrangements #41	52
Mama Said	53
Strange Birds Sing	54
The Garden Emerges	56

SECTION 3: *Spring Tides and Storm Surges*

Photograph: *Root Beer Revival*	60
Antonelli's River Inn	61
Photograph: *Over the Levee*	65

SECTION 4: *Levee Views of the Old River*

from Conversations with Two Rivers	68
White Feathers	69
from Conversations with Two Rivers	70
Family Spondylidea	71
jelli 7	72
Falling Star	73
jelli 8	74
The Night the Moon Fell	75
Ponderings	76
The Dance of the Brown Pelicans	77
Moon Climb	78
Reconciliation	79
Leaf Dreams	80

Lady of the Yucatan	82
Demise of Names	83
jelli 9	84
Night Designs	85
jelli 10	86
Melody of Loons	87
Electric Ice	88
Whitecaps and Ravens	89
Storm Wobbles	90
Dream Flares and Thunder Drops	91
from Conversations with Two Rivers	92
Relative Relativity	93
from Conversations with Two Rivers	94
Raven Legion	95

SECTION 5: *From the Depths of Ancient Coolers*

from Conversations with Two Rivers	98
Ritual in Clay	99
jelli 11	100
The Style of Two Rivers	101
Waiting for Poetry	102
Spumoni Ink	103
from Conversations with Two Rivers	104
Bell Power	105
jelli 12	106
First Fountain	107
Metamorphosis	108
Tree Trance	109
On the Way to Poetry	110
jelli 13	112
Afternoon of Gulls	113
jelli 14	114
Lines and Waves	115
jelli 15	116
Two Rivers' Song	117
Interview with the Author	118
Biographies	122

ix

Introduction: Enhanced Vision

Poetry did not come easily to me.
I first activated my right brain
and then started journal discipline
by writing life lessons.
I now see with my mind, heart,
with eyes newly aware, eyes closed,
with my hands and ears.

To shape poetry, I see and explore
ordinary life in an unorthodox fashion.
At the beach, I look at a common scallop
and examine it there on the dune,
upside-down, inside-out.
My mind sees the shell young and alive
in the salty Gulf of Mexico.
Sees it old and dry
with sheer lace designs etched
in the calcium carbonate.

My heart vision takes a romantic leap.
The scallop changes
to hundreds of heart cockles.
Valentines washed ashore
in a February storm.
A derelict of a man,
sadly wrapped against the storm,
views the broken hearts and mutters
Cajun philosophy to seagulls.

Moon and breeze swirl
wavelets against my ankles,
leave a shiny olive shell resting
just out of reach of the tide.
Newly aware eyes trace the symmetry
of the lettered olive and ponder
the meaning of the zigzag message.

With closed eyes,
I explore the architectural design
of this elegant oval
with five whorls and short spire.
My eyelids provide a backdrop
for a virtual reality show
as oval and zigzags elongate,
foreshorten, fold end over end,
curl up to disappear.

In the glare of high noon,
I touch the surface
of an almost perfect sand dollar.
Nicks and imperfections testify
to the tumble world of the sea,
yet the fragile structure yields
to the slightest pressure,
breaks into halves,
spilling five tiny birds into my palm.
Tactile sensation
becomes enhanced vision.
A poem tingles through my universe.

I hold an eight-inch lightning whelk
against my ear
to hear the roar of wind and ocean
caught in the body whorl
and turreted spiral.
Listening changes
to seeing in the ear canal
where sound and vision mix into a poem.

Later, my hand surrounds
a fast writing pen and ink flows
across the blank journal page.
Ideas and words merge in artistic streams
and create my tribute poem,
"Antonelli's River Inn."

Carlyn Luke Reding

Quintana, Texas
08 February 2003

Editor's Note

To experience the rich language and imagery of *Antonelli's River Inn*, by Carlyn Luke Reding, is to embrace an intimate connection between poet and place. The reader is invited to peer into the poet's memories nourished by the Texas coastal landscape and stroll alongside Reding as she explores and questions personal contemporary issues.

At the heart of this compilation is Antonelli's River Inn — the root beer and ice cream stand, which lends its name to the book's title. This family establishment — built in 1923 by Reding's uncle, Henry Antonelli — began its legendary legacy on a place beside the Brazos River levee. After Antonelli's death in 1980, the stand was moved from the original site to its present location near the famous shrimp boat *Mystery* and Brazosport High School. Despite that relocation, Antonelli's endures the eroding winds of time, and it is with similar resoluteness that the poet pens her works.

Reding draws deeply from years of artistic vision as a director of stage productions. Those years have shaped the movement and timing and sensory details that pulse beneath the surface of her poetry. With subtle ease she ushers ideas along a line, down the page. Subjects turn and pause and appear at the right moment. The poems — both individually as well as collectively — resonate with a southern charm that flows between grace and despair, between fortitude and vulnerability. Reding captures experiences and epiphanies grounded in everyday life; she reveals a woman who laughs as passionately as she weeps.

During the editorial process, a conscientious effort was made to maintain Reding's voice in each of the poems and sections titled "from Conversations with Two Rivers" — which serve to offer insight into the inventive process. As production work on the book evolved, a gentle give-and-take relationship between editor and poet and graphic designer found form. Without question, *Antonelli's River Inn* is a work of beauty — beauty in voice and message, style and language, structure and design.

                                        Susie Kelly Flatau, editor
                                              Austin, Texas

Section One:

1

in the shade
of latticed arches

from Conversations with Two Rivers

The poem, "Bone Dust," is a lament for the loss of the American bison and ultimately the demise of the Native American culture across the continent. Two Rivers, the medicine woman, is the personification of my Native American grandmothers and my pen name when I write in my journals — especially when dream sequences, time warps, and shape-changing entries begin to appear.

I went to Taos, New Mexico, looking for poetic inspiration. I attended a screenwriting workshop led by Jimmy Santiago Baca. Baca read poetry from his *Black Mesa* collection, and during his reading, he casually mentioned that geographical terms make good titles for poetry collections.

When I returned home to Lake Jackson, Texas, I wanted a geographical title for my poetry chapbook. I thought of many options — gulf, delta, creek, levee, beach, and river. I then played around with the titles of Brazos River and Colorado River. Thinking of those two rivers led me to remember my entire educational experience — an education that began at St. Mary's Star of the Sea parochial school. From there, the education of my teen years included Freeport Junior High School and on through Brazosport High School. Upon graduation from high school, I first attended Wharton County Junior College and then moved to and graduated from the University of Texas at Austin. I realized that all of my education had been completed between the Brazos and Colorado Rivers. So I titled my chapbook *Between Two Rivers* and created my pen name of Two Rivers.

A year or so later, my friend Helen Kopczynski (now Helen K. Antonelli) from Albuquerque, New Mexico, sent me Nancy Wood's *Spirit Walker* with illustrations by Frank Howell. When I opened the gift, the cover image was a Native American woman with long gray hair and a bronze sculptured face dressed in a flowing blue gown. A mental image of Two Rivers stared back at me.

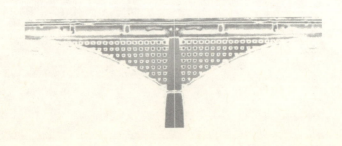

Bone Dust

Medicine woman and buffalo chief,
Two Rivers and Bellow Buff,
stand above the Wings of Crow River.
Partners in the Watching
dignify the altar of memory,
sandbar of bleached bones.

Bone dust rises with the gulf breeze.

Under a fine mist
a flash flood surges down river,
and dust rides
over the south bank
as buffalo stampede.
Flashing Water swallows the herd.
Survivors bellow and moan.

Bone dust rises with the gulf breeze.

Smoke on the prairie, incense of terror.
Scorching Earth chases the buffalo
over the north bank.
Fire flanks the herd.
Jumps the river.
Survivors bellow and moan,
bellow and moan.

Bone dust rises with the gulf breeze.

Iron Horse wails along the river
eating fire, roaring destruction. Halts.
Muffles buffalo protest.
In firecracker imitation
Firestick extends the carnage.
Male, female, and calf
silently sink into memory mounds.

from Conversations with Two Rivers

The poem, "With Each Swing of the Pendulum," is a revision of a poem I wrote titled "Will There Be Enough Time." The poem was my response to Glynn Monroe Irby's poem "The Moment-Arm of Miss Alexia." Glynn is my poetry partner, and my poems often respond to Glynn's poems. Words and phrases seem to jump around between our poems.

Part of my education — like the education of most children in the mid-twentieth century — was completed by imitating the modeling of lessons by my teachers. I learned to imitate and give the teachers the information they wanted on tests.

As an adult, I used that imitation quality of learning in my continuing lifelong education. As well, I began adding variations and products of my imagination to skills in homemaking, classroom instruction, and dramatic production.

When I began to write poetry, I no longer felt the need to imitate. I soon found myself responding to Glynn's work in a manner similar to a process used by Robert Bly and William Stafford as they shared their poetry with each other. Bly explained this sharing technique in a workshop sponsored by the Austin Jung Society.

Another poet friend, Jim Taylor, drove up from Lake Jackson, and we attended the Bly workshop. Jim had previously introduced Glynn and me to Robert Bly's poetry and philosophy during discussions at the Brazosport Poets' Society.

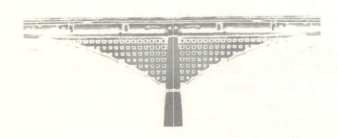

With Each Swing of the Pendulum

celebrate time
as a chameleon shimmies up the cedar
as a hawk swirls above the ravine
as a plane angles down the river

calculate time
to heal the scars on the moon
welcome Aurora dressed in night
as the last plane angles down

calibrate time
for composing the heart
mending the rifts of Apollo
ringing bells along the canal

smooth time
seal the scars of dissonance
explore the mysteries
of the big hand and the little hand
compose the heart once more
as a nighthawk swoops and swirls

caress time
awaking with Aurora
in her dawn's early glow
studying the mystery of hands

harmonize time
heal her heart
ring the bells
as the chameleon shimmies
      green and red

Memory of Fog and Mist

Caught in early morning mist
the savanna tree gleams
while spiders string
glass beads
in the salt cedars
and along the creek
heavy dew highlights
the cantilevered roof.

Somewhere
above the forty acres
the tower looms.
Time erased.
Chimes muffled.

Cables without end
suspend the Golden Gate,
a lavender-rose backdrop
defines the Eiffel Tower,
and gondolas disappear
from canal and lagoon.

Fog smears the edge
of the emerald cliff
above waves, while buoys
clang danger
across channel and over ship
as sweethearts kiss good-bye.

Crossbars

a car backfires
echoes flood the canyon

dogs bark
concealed birds screech
warble and grunt beyond
the weather-beaten cross
reclining on fresh shredded cedar

along the path
aromas steeped in memory
rise in waves blessing the cross —
a carved remnant from a ring of time
studded in knots and screws
waiting for elevation

a sonic boom cracks the sky
echoes flood the canyon

contrails pattern
a wavy-armed cross
above the meditation trail

after a few moments
the crossbars angle off
transform into seagull feathers
floating
then rushing across the sky
whitecaps seeking a distant shore

one cross waits
one cross disappears

jelli 1

on the edge of love field
where time and distance
stalk the unsuspecting
hold your beloved in the heart of the hand
hold the beloved in the hand of your heart

on the edge of love
field where time
and distance stalk
the unsuspecting
hold your beloved
in the heart
of the hand
hold the beloved
in the hand
of your heart
beloved

Clock in the Clouds

first a cloud bank
then a shape
then a face
in the shape
now a clock face

first one time
then another
zoom together
tumble apart

hours
and
minutes
indifferent
to zones
recall
another time
in an altered state of mind

remember
the sacrifice
of the other time
at the altar of the state
that altered the state

remember
recent sacrifice
at the altar of time
at the altar of the mind
in alternating waves of shock
that altered her state
that altered her mind

from Conversations with Two Rivers

When I was still teaching at Brazoswood High School, I shared an earlier version of "Time Honored" with Herb Torres, a colleague and teacher of Spanish in the classroom located next to mine. He nodded and said *el rito* means ritual, and I grinned at my weaving of ideas. I had thought of El Rito as a village but had not thought about the translation of the phrase.

"Time Honored" flows across more than 6,000 years of history, art, architecture, math, chemistry, geology, and my imagination. The ceremonial bowl that graced the coffee table in our Circle Way home in Lake Jackson, Texas, was created by a potter living in El Rito, New Mexico. She uses clay dug in the shadow of the Sangre de Cristos mountains to create her pottery.

The inclusion of I. M. Pei links to discussions with Glynn Irby as he talked about his study of architecture at the University of Houston. I first became aware of the renown architect during these conversations.

When I traveled to Paris, France, I visited the Louvre during the time that Pei's glass pyramids were under construction. Then a trip to the Far East took me to Singapore where I admired Pei's Oversea-Chinese Banking Corporation Centre from my hotel room. Today, I travel to Dallas, Texas, from time to time and I appreciate the Fountain Place (another work by Pei) with its rhomboidal central theme and prismatic glass structure that helps shape the skyline of the city.

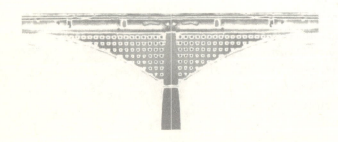

Time Honored

Somewhere in New Mexico
heat sears and bakes earth history
in clay incised with V's and M's
creating *el rito* pottery
suggesting the Sangre de Cristos.

On the coffee table
a pyramid candle burns
within the ceremonial bowl
exhibiting miniature mountains
rough in ceramic elevation.

In Egypt
pyramids
rough to the touch
preserve rituals of civilization
defining ancient art.

Flames ignore
the Pythagorean theory
devouring the geometry of the candle
exposing five plastic trinkets.

In Paris at the Palais du Louvre
I. M. Pei built nouveau glass pyramids
to guard the past
to decorate the present
to salute the future.

from Conversations with Two Rivers

The poem, "Poetry Shards," is dedicated to archaeologists, Raymond Walley and John W. Dunn, Jr., who helped preserve the pottery shards and the Karánkaway lifestyle that are now exhibited in the Brazosport Museum of Natural Science and the Lake Jackson Historical Museum.

"Poetry Shards" reveals the small bit of me — about the time I was in the fourth grade — that once desired to be an archaeologist. It also recalls a time when my sister, Theresa Luke Holmberg, phoned me from another state. She pleaded with me to become an environmental activist and save Shy Pond.

The pond area near downtown Lake Jackson was a former Karánkaway Indian campsite and home to coastal birds and animals. At that time, I was a young wife and mother and I did little to protest the eventual development of Shy Pond.

The poem also presents the spelling of Karánkaway in the style of Roy Bedichek in his book, *Karánkaway Country*. He celebrates the Karánkaway warrior with these words: "... he was fascinated by the sight of the sun submerging itself in the sea. The wonder of sunset over water was too much for the mind of this simple savage. He became as a statue, oblivious to his surroundings, gazing spellbound at the point on the horizon where the waters closed over and quenched this great ball of fire." (pp. 14-15)

Finally, I've written a tribute to my Native American great-grandmothers and grandmothers — whether they were Chitimacha, Choctaw, Cherokee, or Alabama-Coushatta.

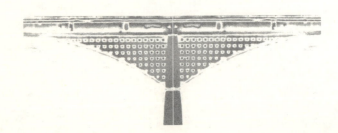

Poetry Shards

Centuries later.
With precision and style
the archaeologist
digs pottery shards
and bones by Shy Pond.
Imagines the grace
of the Karánkaway woman
shaping and molding
gumbo clay and brackish water
from Oyster Creek
into her prized possession.

Imagines this woman
who bequeathed
this puzzle of a pot
to her daughter.
Who later buried
these pieces
beside her mother.

Centuries later
with a shy pen
the poet searches
and shapes
these poetry shards
digging through layers
and shaping them
into a poem.

jelli 2

on this trail
site of once and future seas
a scallop shell
symbol of pilgrims across the ages
rests in a limestone pillow at my feet

on this trail
site of once and
future seas a scallop
shell symbol
of pilgrims
across the ages
rests in a limestone
pillow at my feet

symbol

The Heart in Time

my grandmothers
neglected to tell me
ready or not
sorrow comes
memories vanish
grief grabs the heart
sorrow is strong

my grandmothers
forgot to tell me
eventually
time defeats sorrow
memories return
the heart flourishes
the heart banishes grief

sorrow is strong
but the heart in time is stronger

Rocking Horse Finish

Spit. Polish.
Spit and polish,
imitating Dad. Tyson Luke
applies a military shine to Buck —
horse with a red enamel coat —
combs the yellow mane
of twisted yarn and glides a final swipe
across the flat back with an old bandanna.
With a daddy flourish stuffs the cloth
into his back pocket, admires his handiwork,
looks up when the back door squeaks open.
His mom holds the screened door
controlling the squeakiness.

Ty interprets Violet's vigilant eyes
anticipates her caution.
Don't go down to the creek.
Don't even go to the second level.
Her eyes check the boy, survey the creek,
and return to her small son
as she considers his possible infractions.

Winding past the backyard is Oyster Creek,
off limits to small boys without supervision.
St. Augustine grass extends a golf-course finish
across the second level, where young ones
enter the other world of the creek
shadowed by live oak trees, wild yaupon, and holly.
The steep bank above the second level
creates a secluded canyon
in the otherwise flat coastal plain —
just the place for youthful investigations.

Ty watches Buck's coat glisten
as the sun pops in and out
of anvil-shaped thunderheads.
The boy is not yet a weather-watcher,
but Mom is. She glances at the clouds
before turning back to breakfast dishes.
Then, the phone rings. Ty knows this is his chance.

He quickly pushes and shoves
the rocking horse down to the other world
where boy and horse rock and bump
in the land of raccoon, possum,
owl, alligator, and snake.
The cropped grass and small boy with horse
keep those critters at bay
while cardinal, mockingbird, and jay seek
shelter from a larger critter lurking nearby.

Without warning.
Without red and black flags
of gale or hurricane
the morning glows in a yellow-green twilight.
The green tinged day turns to black.
Violet yells through the screen door.
Tyson Luke come inside this minute,
don't make me come and get you.
The urgency in her voice
pulls the boy away from Buck,
and he scrambles up the steep bank
as the darkness growls low, rumbles slow.

Horse forgotten under stinging raindrops,
Ty reaches the back door as the sudden squall
breaks into a hundred-year monsoon
shedding twenty-six inches
of the best of the Gulf of Mexico
on the Oyster Creek watershed
in the next twenty-four hours.

By morning, Oyster Creek — now a little river —
sprawls through the riverbed
that the Brazos River once called home.
From the back porch Ty and Violet view the creek
as it slowly pushes up the bank and slides downstream
returning the flood back to the Gulf.
As they watch the water rise,
mother explains to son
that long ago the Karánkaway Indians

watched waters rise on this same creek.
They also called it Oyster and ate
its delicacies on the half-shell
and boiled blue crabs in a stew —
called gumbo to this day by Cajun families
along the Southeast Texas coast.

That afternoon his mom prepares gumbo
from a secret family recipe and
the boy remembers his rocking horse
left in the rain down by the creek.
He cries tears only a small boy can cry.
Violet cries with him.

Boy and mom search for Buck when the water recedes,
but they never find him. Soon they move away
from the creek, and Tyson Luke promises
to remember Buck — his horse that rocked but couldn't swim.

Years later another boy plays too close
to the creek during a Texas drought.
He investigates the now dry lower level
and finds the horse in a tangle of branches
above mud-stage. The new boy
rescues the rocking horse, but it falls apart
as he carries it up the slope. His mom
shakes her head at the barnacled pieces
and stacks them on the curb to be recycled.

Early the next morning
Theresa, patroness of things broken,
jogs past the puzzle pieces of rocking horse.
She stops. Jogs back
and examines the discarded toy,
touches the dry barnacles.
Then runs home and returns in her car
arranges the pieces of horse carefully in a box
takes him home and places the box
on a high shelf in the garage.
More years pass before Buck and his cardboard home

move from the garage in Flag Lake
to Waco. His revival begins.

Theresa, now great-aunt to Eleanor,
plans to restore the horse
to celebrate Eleanor's first Christmas.
So Great-aunt Theresa and Great-uncle Bill scrub
and sand and paint the horse parts.
Bill masters the puzzle. Re-establishes the horse.
Theresa sews and glues the mane in place,
then combs it with her fingers.

Proud and handsome — a full three hands high —
the horse waits nervously
under the branches of the Christmas tree
in the Park Lane living room.
His piano-grade enamel gleams
on green rockers, blue legs, red head, and body.
The soft, yellow mane flows
over his neck around blue handles.

Eleanor's face lights up with Christmas charm
when she notices the rocking horse.
She baby-steps straight to him.
Takes possession. Instinctively,
names him Buc, his own age-old name.
Straddles his strong, flat back for a test ride
on the hardwood floor. She rocks wildly,
as wild as any boy ever rode a rocking horse.

Buc blinks and looks around. Glimpses
the tall fence surrounding the backyard,
no creek or bayou or arroyo in sight.
A slight smile decorates his face.
He silently thanks Tyson Luke for good times.
Blesses the boy who rescued him.
Winks at his patroness of broken things.
Promises to watch after Eleanor
keeping her safe from harm —
in his new playroom domain.

from Conversations with Two Rivers

This poem, "Memorywalk," is a travelogue of my trip to the Far East and several trips to Europe. I have created a journal entry of a pretend day of adventures to Venice, Paris, Taos, Kuala Lumpur, Vienna, Mont-Saint-Michel and back to Paris.

After listening to a constant stream of motorcycles outside my hotel in Florence, Italy, the noise curfew in Vienna was a pleasant surprise.

The Texas-sized rainstorm shocked me as we drove through the countryside from Mont-Saint-Michel to downtown Paris. The bus driver said the streets near the Paris Hilton were flooded and he would be unable to stop at the hotel. So, he dropped me on the Champs-Elysees near the Arch of Triumph in rain, wind, and lightning. A taxi came along about twenty minutes later. The cab driver had no trouble driving to the Hilton, and I had enough francs to pay the fare.

The poem is also a memory guide as at least ten lines will be the basis for ten new poems. A new poetry book looms on the horizon as I review my photo albums, journals, and relive some of the adventures.

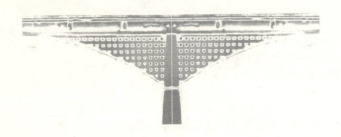

Memorywalk

She documents adventure on film
but we, her blue and white jogging shoes,
record all her steps.

We watch pigeons squabble in St. Mark's Square,
inhale aromas in an alpine village,
light candles in Notre Dame,
ponder frescos in an eighth-century chapel,
meditate in the shadow of Taos Mountain,
hike across the mesa to the edge of the Rio Grande gorge.

We never jog.

After a nap, she leaves us
outside the mosque in Kuala Lumpur
but remembers us on the way out.
Then buys an ice cream cone and almost misses the bus.

As the noise curfew uncurls across Vienna,
we listen while quiet blankets the city.
At midnight on les Champs-Elysees,
after a day trip to Mont-Saint-Michel,
we wait for a taxi in the rain.

Finally, she sleeps.
We compare soles
and then we sleep.

from Conversations with Two Rivers

This poem, "A Celebration of the Feminine," honors the imagination and work of dedicated NASA scientists and pilots who created the United States space program.

It especially celebrates the women in the program and their leadership — as represented by Colonel Eileen Collins, first woman shuttle commander, on the STS-93 *Columbia* in July 1999.

I have also written a tribute to *Challenger*. That particular poem, "Wreath of Dolphins," (p. 29) was penned shortly after the tenth anniversary of the *Challenger* disaster. I was watching a television show that recounted memorial services across the nation. The last scene viewed was of a wreath floating in the Atlantic — with dolphins swimming nearby as a salute, a natural benediction.

On February 1, 2003, I watched in stunned silence as the space shuttle *Columbia* disintegrated across the television screen. I knew I would write a second ending for the "Wreath of Dolphins" so that the poem also celebrates the heroes of *Columbia*.

My Brazoswood students and I created a *Challenger* fund to purchase memorials to be placed on the Brazoswood High School campus in Clute, Texas. We collected enough money to purchase and plant seven Flowering Plum trees in the back courtyard. The trees bloom in January, usually during the week of the 28th. The blooms now honor both *Columbia* and *Challenger*.

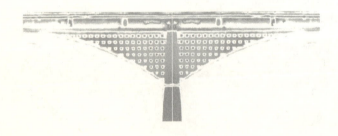

A Celebration of the Feminine

Anticipation erupts in shouts of jubilation
at the *Columbia* sighting
just as Columbus shouted at the sight of land
at the sight of the new world
as the Santa Maria sailed west.

Exclamations echo
through the hills
following the flight of the shuttle
billowing a buttery trail
of yellow plasma
etching the dark sky
propelling the spacecraft
horizon to horizon
high above Zilker Park
high above the granite capitol.

The moon shines congratulations.
Under the lady's command,
Columbia winks back
landing at Kennedy Space Center
a mere twenty minutes later.

Saturday Morning at *Sainte-Mere-Eglise*

Dedicated to Senator George McGovern
In memory of Dr. Stephen E. Ambrose

Operation Overlord

      June 6, 1944. D-Day.
Normandy. Invasion beaches.
Omaha. Utah. Gold. Juno. Sword.
Pegasus Bridge.
Major John Howard's gliders.
Pointe de Hoc.
Lt. Col. James E. Rudder's allee.
La Roche-Guyon.
Field Marshal Rommel's command post.
Colonel Hans von Luck and his panzers.
Officers and Gentlemen.
Pawns in a world-class game of chance.

Operation Ambrose

      July 17, 1987.
Overnight train, Innsbruck to Paris.
American students stuff backpacks
with *The Longest Day* and *Pegasus Bridge*.
D-Day codes:
Overlord and Ham and Jam,
agitate sleep and invade dreams.

      July 18, 1987.
Paris to Bayeux by overland coach.
Rain falls at Utah Beach.
Students run for the coach
where American soldiers
once ran for cover.
Tears fall at Omaha Beach
where white crosses mark
the final home of the brave.

Words carved in marble
salute Jews and Christians alike:
Think not only upon their passing

but the glory of their spirit.
Through the gate of death they pass
to their joyful resurrection.
In '44, American paratroopers jumped
at Ste.-Mere-Eglise, and years later
Red Buttons jumped in the movie
The Longest Day.
In '87, the Romanesque church
of a thousand years shimmers,
a jewel of Norman ingenuity.

Stained glass windows,
stacks of votive candles,
and age-old aroma of incense
intrigue and mystify.
Haunting melodies
unleashed from ancient pipes
reverberate about the nave
previewing the Sunday celebration.

Altar society ladies whisper,
Bonjour, mon Dieu.
Genuflect.
Cross themselves.
Arrange fresh lilies
and stretch the starched altar cloth.
They genuflect again
before polishing the pews.

The music ceases.
The altar society genuflects once more
then retreats to the sacristy.

Outside, the sun still splashes
Rue de Eisenhower and
a mannequin and a tangled parachute
cling to the bell tower — a sad memory
of the grim beginning of D-Day
and a final tribute in cloth and silk
to the valiant American liberators
and their courageous defense of liberty.

Misappropriation of Oleanders

Civil defense wardens of World War II —
deactivated guardians of the coastal village
trade hard hats and ration books
for white gloves and straw hats
reactivating the garden club
in the exchange.

No longer collecting pots and pans
or unmentionables for Project Victory
the ladies siphon nickels and dimes
from household budgets
and extract fives and tens
from businessmen for Project Oleander.

With the bank account
flourishing in civic pride
fifty oleander bushes arrive
destined for garden plots along
Plantation Drive and city hall.

But overnight
sabotage
disturbs the newfound peace.
In subterfuge and darkness
pranksters plant the lanky bushes
flowering pink and white
on private property
out on the highway
where mystery and aroma
still linger on the breeze.

In the Shadow of Los Alamos

one day
one cat
one whiskered miniature shamu
bianca bella maria cecillia sforza
bathes her black and white coat
morning night noon
no mirror necessary

one october day
one family car
black and white '57 buick
two-door two-toned delight
desertion
disillusion
despair
reflect in the rearview mirror

one day in hiroshima
one bomb

later
one day in tokyo
one man
one face
one-half black
one-half white
no mirror necessary

Underground Undertow

Unleashed from ashen tributaries
pedestrians
pushing forward
jam and bloat the swift river
seeking
hidden channels
downstream.

Blank faces
float in currents
of black trench coats
with ebony boots
rushing against the flow.

Streams of eyes focus
on routine
missing red and yellow
neon eddies
hearing none
of the conversation
splashing the shores
of the subterranean city.

Wreath of Dolphins

Two women
five men
seeking heights of space
its mysteries to conquer
challenge human imperfection,
rockets, and gravity.
Fortune redirects the mission
hurls their roaring shuttle
to quiet ocean depths.

The nation shudders
in disbelief
in despair
as teachers cry
beside the children.

Ten years later
memorials honor *Challenger*
across land and sea.
In a helicoptic downdraft
the final wreath drops to the Atlantic.
Then seven dolphins
salute the lost.
Splash their benediction
surrounding the circle of flowers.

  Seven years
  and four days later
  Columbia dissolves
  along a path of fire and ice
  as seven stars blaze
  across the day sky
  etching their souls through time.

from Conversations with Two Rivers

My parents taught me to beachcomb on Sunday afternoons, to admire the porpoise, and to watch the weather. Daddy always cautioned: "Look out for sudden squalls off the gulf and don't get caught on the beach in high tides."

"Camera Works" is a father-mother-daughter poem that begins with my granddaughter Eleanor at the beach with her parents. It continues with her mom, Elizabeth, playing at the beach with John and me. I in turn play on the beach with Earl and Violet. The last stanza ponders where and with whom my mother played at the beach. She probably played at Sargent Beach in Matagorda County, but I don't know and never thought to ask her.

The poem reflects on the importance of beach outings across three generations. In the days before television and fast food, beach activities such as swimming, collecting shells, and making a driftwood fire completed a Sunday afternoon. Later, we would ignore the small silver screen and simply go to the beach. Sometimes we spent part of Christmas Eve day on the beach; sometimes we spent part of Christmas day, New Years day, or Super Bowl Sunday on the beach.

I have walked the beach in all months of the year, in the wake of hurricanes and blue northers, but my favorite months for beachcombing are October and February.

October walks remind me of a short educational course I once took — "The Fauna and Flora of the Brazosport Beach and Jetty." Dr. Dorothea Mangum taught the course on site — in field trip fashion. On the edges of Christmas Bay, we dug quahog clams, and I was introduced to anemones attached to the granite rocks of the Quintana jetty along the Old River channel.

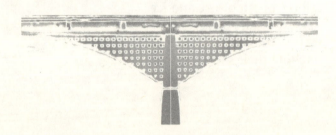

Camera Works

Surfside Beach.
A digital camera clicks
Eleanor Anne clasping strong hands
as she laughs and jumps the waves,
a wild-thing shrieking —
Beach, Beach — as porpoise play
beyond the breakers.

Quintana Beach.
A Polaroid clicks
Elizabeth Lee and Theresa Lynn,
sun-seeking anemones,
dancing the waves
clinging to strong hands.
Porpoise imitate their antics.

Bryan Beach.
A Brownie clicks
Carlyn Ann grasping strong hands,
a wild-thing jumping and splashing
above the salty waves.
Porpoise circle
then sail away.

No camera clicked.
No one remembers
where Violet laughed
and jumped the waves
imitating the porpoise.
No one remembers
who held Mama's hands.

jelli 3

red moon pales
through blue nights
longing for time
and the ritual of seasons
while frankincense sparks
memory into the chalice
of the soul.

red moon pales
through blue nights
longing for time and
the ritual of seasons
while frankincense
sparks memory into
the chalice of the soul

seasons

Back to the Beginning

what if
two walk on the jetty
      in raindrops

what if
drops change to swans' feathers and
      wrap them in downy fog

what if
feathers mix with snowflakes and
      dazzle them in blizzard light

what if
blinding sensuality
      melts the tempest
           and washes the two out to sea?

Section Two:

2

root beer
and painted rocks

from Conversations with Two Rivers

This poem recalls my first snow. The night before the snow, I attended a basketball game with my dad, Earl Luke. The gym was on the campus of Freeport High School located on West Fourth Street. As we left the bright lights and warmth of the gym, sleet was beginning to coat the cars and parking lot. This was my first sleet, and I was impressed.

The next day, Mama and Daddy were excited about the early morning snow, and my sister, Theresa, and I joined in their holiday-like cheer. However, once outside we were cold. Building Frosty the Snowman was not much fun.

I was glad to return indoors to the warmth of space heaters and I watched the rest of the day through frosted windows. Icicles hung from the eaves and dripped in the afternoon. They lasted until the next day.

The Port Café faced Toby's Hardware and Brown's clothing store across Park Avenue. Gautreaux's Cleaners and the First National Bank were the café's neighbors at opposite ends of the block. The Tarpon Inn rested against the Old River levee at the north end of the avenue and watched fishermen and townspeople frequent the café in all seasons.

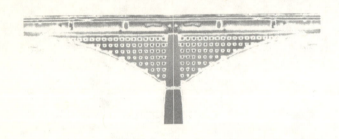

First Coffee First Snow

Early morning snow flurries
surprise Old River shrimp boats
and the salt grass prairie.
Sticky flakes drizzle the bays and beaches.

Inside the Port Café, idled fishermen
guzzle first coffee and recall first snow.
A few blocks away,
Daddy stirs his first coffee and shouts,
Wake-up. It's snowing. It's the winter of 1949.
Mama skips her coffee.
Layers us in sweaters, coats, hats, gloves, and excitement.
Then, roly-poly creations threaten
the edges of the hall mirror.
Triple-socks
stretch our shoes.
Snow boots
exist in Mama's imagination,
not on the Texas Gulf Coast.

Outside, we waddle and slip
and roll a penguin-sized snowman
as arctic air sears noses, insides, and toes.
Later, we salute the grass-stained statue
melting in a patch of trampled mud.

The winter of 1950 spends the night on the Old River.
Wraps the shrimp boats in crystal nets.
Ensnares the salt grass in icy webs.
Next morning, at the Port Café,
local folks savor first coffee.
Recall first snow.

from Conversations with Two Rivers

When the Freeport Sulphur Company started new operations at Bryan Mound, a part of my family relocated from the Weeks Island sulphur and salt mine areas of south Louisiana to Freeport, Texas.

Sons and daughters of my great-grandparents, William and Lumina Gagneaux Tyson, made the move. These folks, my great-aunts and uncles and grandparents, were members of the Hall, Fields, Keller, Tyson, and Luke families.

My grandparents, J. Conley and Theresa Tyson Luke, lived on West Broad near the icehouse when I knew them. Grandpa Luke was part of the operating crew that serviced and ran the company switch engine "FSC 1" until he retired. The Luke daughters married into the Ruddick, Webb, Mallory, Craig, Harvey, Stone, Meriwether, and Antonelli families. My dad, Earl, married Violet Harris. His brother Herman never married.

The Tarpon Inn — a landmark of Freeport, Texas, for over forty years — was built by the Freeport Sulphur Company around 1912. The hotel with its English tavern façade was anchored on the levee of the Brazos River and faced Park Avenue on the south. Pink and white oleanders edged the parking lot and the path over the levee that led to the river.

Grandma Luke cautioned her grandchildren, "Don't eat oleander leaves! They're poisonous." I didn't.

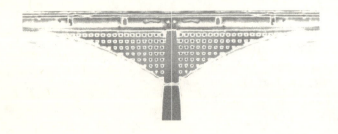

The Tarpon Inn

I never went into the inn,
I never saw a soul enter.
So who stayed there?

One little girl lived in the side apartment,
but I never visited.
I don't know if she lived with anyone.
I never saw anybody with her.
Maybe she had a cat.
I never saw it.

One day the inn fell down.
No, it was not by hurricane.
Some rich men wanted a strip mall.

Now the Tarpon Inn and the girl are gone,
and the mall is boarded up.
Maybe
I never saw the inn.
Maybe
the little girl didn't live there with her cat.

from Conversations with Two Rivers

The ideas for "Tugs and Barges" began in Dr. Robert Cotner's history class at the University of Texas in 1963 as we studied the twentieth century South. My final paper was on the history of the intracoastal canal. The class projects were so important to Dr. Cotner that he provided us with access to the stacks in the Tower usually reserved for graduate students.

"Tugs and Barges" was originally written for my final exam in Mr. Richard Wilcher's creative writing class at Brazosport College in 1972. I told Mr. Wilcher on the last day of class that writing poetry was too hard for me. It demanded too much of my soul, and as wife and mother, I did not have the energy required for such creativity. It would be twenty years before I wrote poetry again.

In the 1990s, some of Mr. Wilcher's former students — including me — created the Brazosport Poets' Society. The group met once a month for several years at the Brazosport Center for the Arts and Sciences. This is where I first read "Tugs and Barges" to other poets. Some of our members were Jo Lynne Roye, Eddie Weems, Glenn McBride, Rhonda Moran, Jim Taylor, Eric McIntyre, and Glynn Irby.

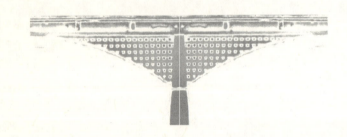

Tugs and Barges

Night and day, tugboats and barges
        churn the intracoastal waterway
                from Brownsville to Jacksonville.
        The unexpected lurks around the next curve.
Anxious men keep watch. In fog a possible collision.
            No time.   No room to maneuver.
      Grounding on an oyster reef spoils the bay.

                Combustible cargo and flood tides
                      complicate
   slipping the locks on the Brazos and the Colorado.
        Unwieldy barges splinter
            and bash wooden retaining walls.
        Between steel gates,
   a scrape threatens   explosion.

            Veteran canalmen
                navigate the barges.
    Sand and shell and fuel and food
            float in rhythms
                of the tidelands.
    Moody storm-framed skies mist
        the canal and salt grass prairies.
Bankside cattle
        watch the boats and birds
in avian ebb and flow.
   A meadowlark,   some red-winged blackbirds,
three roseate spoonbills,   one green heron and a great-blue
    relocate across   the canal.
    Twilight's hint of fire
  mesmerized the Karánkaway,
gilds the birds, cattle, tugs, and barges.

Sometimes on Valentine's Day

I walk Quintana beach
in search of heart cockles.
Today I survey the backdrop
of winter sky, Crow, jetty, and beach.
I listen to winter's symphony
of Crow, wave, buoy, and wind.

Crow sits beside me on the granite.
We explore the upper reaches of a tidal pool.
There salinity and warmth
caress graceful anemones.
Safe in the moment,
their delicate flower faces follow the sun.
Oysters perma-glued
in the damp stony crevasses
court security across the ages.
A blue crab slips beneath the surface
in the liquid spotlight.

A new wave disintegrates on the rocks.
Its salty remains fall on Crow and me.
Holy water from an ancient blessing. Yet,
the anemones withdraw into nondescript blobs;
the oysters ignore the tremor;
the crab disappears.

Blessing or not
the wave dissolves the scene.
A millennium evolves into eternity.

A shiver of remembering washes over me
and Crow flaps his wings.
Together, we search for the soul of the pool.
Crow's eye becomes dark and liquid like the pool.
I can't separate the two.
My inner eye senses
a cold dark passage
              stretching
                        through eternity and beyond.
    Crow blinks.

From School to Other Times

Buoys clang above channel waves
tucked behind the west levee
as signal bells ring, ending sixth period
at Brazosport High School.
Exactly six minutes later
a dozen yellow and black buses
roll away from the parking lot.
    The wake of dust settles
    over the Old River.

In the nine miles in twenty minutes
to Lake Jackson
we pass the skating rink
and the Tradewind and Surf drive-in movies
flaunting romance of geography with that of the stars.
Cows graze in pastures beside chemical plants, and
we stop routinely at the Missouri-Pacific tracks
before crossing bridges
over the barge canal and boggy Flag Lake.

The left turn down Plantation Drive
zooms to other times
    when oaks shaded Eagle Island Plantation
    and sun and rain sprinkled cotton.
    After war and neglect and hurricanes,
    Eagle Island retreated into the forest.

    Later another high school, Brazoswood,
    will grow where once the cotton grew.

And then we pass the Dairy Queen.
I'm almost home.

jelli 4

on the edge of love field
a delicate kite
a dragonfly
hangs
in the wake
of a white crane

on the edge
of love field
a delicate kite
a dragonfly
hangs
in the wake
of a white crane

on the edge
of love field
a delicate kite
a dragonfly
hangs
in the wake
of a white crane

Plums to Pines

Seventeen Desoto Parish miles still ride
the hills from Mansfield to Grandpa's farm.
Once plum trees bloomed
there beside the red barn scattering
white petals over scruffy cotton fields
and sugarcane sweetened the bottom.
Curving away from Pelican and pointing
toward Wallace cemetery and Pleasant Hill,
the road separated barn from farmhouse.

Saturday mornings, Aunt Bessie swept and
mopped the wrap-around porch. After chores
Grandpa parked the pickup and rested
in shade and shadows. Around back
below the kitchen steps hens scratched
and the scary rooster crowed.
Farther out, the stock pond
lured boys beyond the rule.
No Fishing on Sunday.

Boys caught in the act,
wonder what they did wrong.
Later, civil engineers dismantle the barn
to pave and widen the road.
Forestry rangers follow — planting pine trees
in the petal-covered fields and redefine the farm.
Then under guardian fire-towers,
green-and-white, diamond-cut
signs announce the Tree Farm.

Today, all signs have vanished.
No boys fish the pond.

French Quarter Boutique

River of swift snow melt
delivering life to the desert
flows in finger-pointed secrets
in ever darker layers of longing
hiding behind gold stars.
Rays of sandalwood
essence of woman and her fan
stretch the rising sun
above the walled river city,
still clinging to the mauve and
deep purples of the damask night.

Waves of vetiver and lavender
reach out to Rue Royale
enticing Violette inside the shop.
There a translucent negligee
reveals a transparent gown
glimmering her imagination.
She touches the lingerie
wondering —
then dismisses temptation
remembering
Madame Irene's treasured
trousseau advice.
> *All you need is a lavender ribbon*
> *and some vetiver cologne.*

In valleys of black-and-white taffeta
in hills of black velvet two women wait
in nineteenth century photographs
facing each other with curls tight,
some loose.

As the twentieth century spreads
into storms beyond onion steeples,
birds of smoke streak the sky and a candle gleams
behind two crosses etching stained-glass windows.
Meanwhile, Man and Woman
turn toward the rainbow
anchored in the Marmalade Glacier
glittering across Rose Mountains.

Points Further East

The night traveler
navigates Houston's rivers of traffic,
enters the easterly flow
leaving red ribbons in his wake.

Long lines of light diminish at dawn
revealing highways and byways with bridges
over swamp and bayou, river and creek.
Overhead an eastbound plane from Hobby
catches the jet stream
racing the traveler to points further east.

Psyche, the traveler's constant companion,
hovers high in swirls of a Vivaldi concerto
spinning from the silver disk
hidden under the dashboard.

She narrates a running commentary
of the plane's long view
of the Big Thicket, the Natchez Trace,
the Blue Ridge Mountains, the Atlantic.
The plane vanishes in a cloud bank.

She shrugs.
Then itemizes county seats,
state capitals, churches and universities
for the traveler.
Together, they count counties into states.

She views the birthplaces
of presidents and generals
and the liberty bell and
weeps at the tombs of the famous,
the common man, and the Unknown Soldier.

The traveler checks the compass,
the car veers east.
He wonders what is east of the point.
From her realm of music,
Psyche smiles and keeps the secret.

jelli 5

on the edge of love field
atoms and electrons
balance
the equation
of longing
desire completes
the orbit of the beloved

on the edge
of love field
atoms and electrons
balance the equation
of longing
desire completes
the orbit
of the beloved

desire

Acequias in Shadow

Taos Mountain
Mother of the Pueblo
initiates the Watching ceremony
under streams of clouds.

She thunders.
> *Observe my curves and diagonal lines*
> *touch these sharp edges and stony patterns*
> *survey this memory monument of waves*
> *witness the Piñon forest —*
> *reflection of ancient oceans.*

Sensuous under her quilts,
Taos sends showers and snow melt
through the acequias
her sacred canals
to the edge of existence.

She cajoles.
> *Come to me.*
> *Surrender.*

I bow and swing her censer.
Smell the incense.
Take her chalice.
Drink the wine.

jelli 6

while bruises and teeth marks
still mar her body
she divorces the love of her life
later on bourbon street
solitary
eyes overcast
he disappears in mardi gras

while bruises and teeth marks still mar her body she divorces the love of her life later on bourbon street **solitary eyes** overcast he disappears in mardi gras

overcast

Leaving Los Alamos

In shadows
under walking rain
dormant volcanoes
laboratories and radiation
etch the desert.

Under thunder
in explosive light
carved across the Sangre de Cristos
mesas echo traditions
of Taos Pueblo
St. James
and St. Francis.

Sleeping Arrangements #41

Daybreak on the banks of the Old River
    finds the shrimping village
    stretching and listening
    for the roar of Surfside breakers.
    Hears clatter of construction downstream.
On the salt grass prairie fertilized
    by government contracts and deferments,
    the Chemical Company
    expands and sprouts styrene, chlorine,
    bromine, and magnesium.
Troops in hard hats
    comb the beach looking for sabotage,
    walk the jetties searching for submarines.
Soldiers of Vital Industry
    work day, evening, and graveyard shifts.
    Sleep in rented beds.
Sheets changed three times a day, if weather permits.
Others sleep on shrimp boats, in private cars,
in tents under the railroad trestle.
Some share chicken coops.
Across the garden from Grandma Theresa's chickens,
    Mama and Daddy sleep in her storage shed.
    Cardboard-papered walls
    and tar-chinked door resist blue northers.
    Screens on the door and window halt
    mosquitoes and encourage the gulf breeze.
Cozy in boomtime luxury,
    Earl and Violet greet St. Valentine's Day
    with no thought of war,
    with no thought of me.
    My November birthday does not surprise them.

Eighteen days later,
    the Japanese bomb Pearl Harbor.

Mama Said

a good talk can cure
almost anything.
Remember talking
is an activity of the mouth,
but listening
is an activity of the heart.
An understanding friend is always there.
Don't count calories
when you lunch with friends.
Laughter makes the world.
Friends are like wine.
Sometimes you just need a shoulder.
Sometimes you don't.
Great minds think.
Make time to do stuff.
I mean stuff, not work.
When it comes to bonding, do it.
Slumber parties keep you young.

And God laughed.
And sometimes Mama cried.

Strange Birds Sing

I
Song of Ireland
sing of the green.
A wee bit of Erin
came by here today.
Along the banks
of the creek called Oyster,
pastels of sunrise
arouse neighborhoods
with cups of coffee
and steaming dew.
Spanish moss draped
in towers of oaks
drizzles
grey-green salutes
to full-bosomed azaleas
winking mauve and magenta
shadowed flirtation.
So strange the day.
So, strange birds sing.

II
Song of Ireland
sing of the green.
A wee bit of Tara
came by here today.
The soft mist of evening
glistens
my hair, face, and hands
as I pace Circle Way
down to the church.
There, sprinkles
sparkle and trace the length
of the brick campanile
and emerald-laced daffodils
kneel near the gate.
So strange the day.
So, strange birds sing.

III
Song of Ireland
sing of the green.
After candle-lit Vespers
of incense
blessing
and bells,
a wee bit of Shannon
came by here tonight.
A mix of dense fog
from the gulf
and green mercury vapor
haloes
the Celtic cross
caught on the steeple.
So strange the day.
So, strange birds sing.
Song of Ireland
sing of the green.
His grace, Saint Patrick,
came by here today.

The Garden Emerges

circle after circle
too many to count
in gold and pink and purple
and blue and green
smeared and squiggled
counting all the roads and pathways
ancient and modern
across the planet
across the galaxy
across creation —

circles of atoms
carrying electrons and their trails
tying us together in links
and strings and theory
in our search
for the garden of eden —

silly humans
humankind
kind humans who sometimes think war
practice war in the age-old search
for the garden
silly humans if only they would look inward —

to the in-mind seas
seeing in mind where the garden exists
has always existed
since that moment of expulsion
by the creator
or maybe by ourselves
for what parent would
ever really expel the children —

the garden is right here
even as heaven
the garden thrives in the right brain
protected by the left brain
and our human eyes
look outward
at our human lives —

once the left brain is subdued
and the right brain works
to integrate the left
and our human eyes close
to look inward
letting the eyes of the soul
lead the way —

the garden emerges

Section Three:

3

spring tides and storm surges

Root Beer Revival, 1981

Antonelli's River Inn

I
Remember Antonelli's carnival sight
of painted rocks, gaudy signs, and neon lights
as root beer, crepe paper,
and a Neapolitan necklace
tease the imagination.
In paint and plywood,
red, green, and yellow diamond cutouts
produce perfect pendants on the shutters,
add bold broaches to the levee fence.

A pecan tree and a fragrant chinaberry
shade the latticed arcade.
Architecture unusual on the Gulf Coast
requires a second look. Inside
orange and blue crepe paper swags
circle the ceiling and sway in the breeze,
while the cash register rings
salutes to the root beer king.
Gleaming candy jars
soft-drink bottles and exotic cigar boxes
cram shelves in the cool green interior.
Tempting ice cream posters
proclaim sweet hand-dipped delights.
Uncle Henry's original design announces,
Keg Root Beer.
From the depths of ancient coolers
ice-flected mugs emerge to surround
the frothy brew, recipe secret and unique.
Thirst awaits time's tested ritual,
one dripping-wet mug placed in the cooler
replaces each customer's frosted one.
Then open keg's spigot, fill mug to overflowing,
close spigot, wait. Foam and carbonation
dissipate. Fill the second time
with foam just to the brim. Then,
a common man's fanfare and finale
quenches thirsty man.

II
Lady Borden's Ice Cream.
A double-dipped butter pecan cone sounds good.
Proprietor Antonelli's eyes twinkle encouragement.
If time permits, reminisce and savor the River Inn's delights.
Conversationalist Antonelli remembers Freeport as a cow town,
as in India favored cattle roamed the streets.
To discipline cattle from yards and gardens
each home flounced a white picket fence
like Scarlett in a new petticoat.

Henry laments the Tarpon Inn,
once a gracious lady above the downtown esplanade,
before a shopping center coveted her park and river view.
Mr. Antonelli recalls the Brazos River before the earthen dam.
The levee outback
contained spring flood tides and autumn storm surges.
The river's offerings of sun-dried driftwood
teased the treasure seekers.
Now the levee restrains the polluted Old River and
still holds back the storm surge.

A veteran of World War I, Private Antonelli denounces
trenches, mustard gas, and troop transports.
Winks as saucy French maids flash in focus.
World War II demanded
new chemical reactions, towers, and flares.
Boomtown excitement balanced the equations.
The Sulphur Company brought the first boom
some years before World War I.
Raconteur Henry recounts
World War II housing shortages
as vital industry began to breathe round the clock.
Unhoused workers slept shift by shift in boarding houses,
in cars and chicken coops, and under the railroad trestle.
Food and gas rationing along with Civil Defense drills
were all too commonplace.
Uncommon Antonelli's had ice cream for sale.

III
Just sip the root beer
as Uncle Henry discusses
morals, ethics, politics, weather.
He insists young people
acquire an education
search for quality in lifelong mates.
To girls in gingham, pigtails, and ribbons,
he suggests a hard working man,
one who doesn't drink, gamble, or smoke.
To boys rolling the afternoon papers,
he recommends a sweet, young lady,
a good cook, one willing to keep the house
and mind the children.
Beware idle women who smoke and play bridge.
Uncle Henry never discussed
liquor laws, prohibition, or bootlegging
in front of me, but I know he deplores
welfare laws and politicians.

Henry's eighty now and lonesome
since Aunt Daisy died.
Some days the root beer stand is open.
Some days not.
If the weather is good,
he oysters on Christmas Bay.
When horsetails in the sky signal foul weather,
Henry knows how to batten down.
He survived the 1900 Storm.
While the stand is open
Uncle Henry rakes leaves or repaints the diamonds,
hangs out the wash or mows the grass on the levee.
Chores cease — he serves the customer.
A frosted root beer.
A double-dipped cone.
There's no charge for the listening.

IV

Seductive coastal architecture sings a Siren melody.
First, cameras, then paintbrushes answer
as watercolors, oils, pastels, and acrylics
two-step, or waltz, or polka across stretched canvas.
Glossy photos drip and shimmy into treasures
while signed and framed canvases hang around the globe.
Then, Siren summons Air Italia
and my search for latticed arches
with Neapolitan necklaces begins.
Soon, a blue-and-white traffic sign proclaims
Roma. Here across the piazza
from the Pantheon, architectural relic of Imperial Rome,
Antonelli's Bar toasts the twentieth century.
Fading arch, dusky color, liquid refreshment all wrong.

South, sings the Appian Way
to the Autostradda del Sol
toward Monte Cassino, Naples, and Capri.
Lounging under umbrella pines at Sorrento
overlooking oleanders at Pompeii,
Antonelli's cousins display
newly wrought Neapolitan necklaces
of fresh lemon and orange clusters
strung in stainless steel accents.
Umbrellas — red, blue, green, and yellow
catch the breeze and shade carnival competition
under the Mediterranean sun.

I drink lemonade garnished with two tiny icebergs,
translucent lemon slice, with no ice-flecks.
I lick the creamy *gelate*
served in a waffle cone warm from the griddle.
Here Antonelli's ancestral roots and tree stand secure
while branches sway to the Siren's song
in the shadow of the glaciered Alps,
in sun-splashed Sirmioni on Lake Guarda,
in sun-vibrant Venice on the Adriatic.
Listening in any language remains the same.

Over the Levee, 1981

Section Four:

4

levee views
of the old river

from Conversations with Two Rivers

Again in "White Feathers," I use the spelling of Karánkaway as Bedichek does in *Karánkaway Country,* published by the University of Texas Press, 1974. This book is one of my favorite gifts to give newcomers to the Texas Gulf Coast, and I often mark my favorite passages in the book before I give it away.

One passage about meadow larks is in the introduction on pages xxii-xxiv. "The meadow lark is not the hearing kind....This bird never quite surrenders his own personality to the regimented mob....meadow larks — all represent a way of looking at the world — one of the avenues of reality, if you will."

My mother, my very own naturalist, taught me to recognize horsetails in the sky as she taught me "hurricane preparedness."

In 1961, Hurricane Carla pushed a couple of inches of water into our South Magnolia home in Lake Jackson. We lost very little to the rising water, because Mama taught us to move our treasures and valuables to closet shelves and counter tops before we ran from the storm.

We returned to Carla's aftermath and counted ourselves lucky compared to so many others in the Brazosport area and along the Texas coast.

The strong memory of Hurricane Carla always sticks inside us, and we especially remember when another hurricane threatens anywhere, not just the Texas coast. The damp mustiness from Carla would return time and again to Daddy's home after hard rains. We didn't notice it in the high heat of summer or the dry cold of winter.

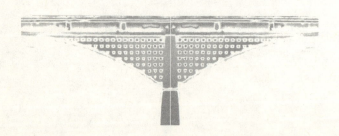

White Feathers

The Karánkaway
watch the sky and
read the cloud ceremony
when white feathers float
into horsetails
expanding the sky
above hill, prairie, and gulf.

They know the sky.
They plan their retreat.

Harbingers of rain
weave the cloud ceremony.
Horsetails trail across the sky
fly sidesaddle with the wind
forecasting gales
predicting the hurricane.

The Karánkaway watch
the clouds change.
They know the sky.

from Conversations with Two Rivers

During the early 1970s, I was a guest columnist for *The Brazosport Facts* and wrote "Arti-Facts" for Marguerite Davidson while she and her husband Jock vacationed in climes cooler than coastal Texas. Marguerite initiated "Arti-Facts" to report on the weekly activities of the Brazosport Museum of Natural Science in downtown Lake Jackson.

My poem, "Family Spondylidea," refers to information in "Arti-Facts" that I wrote on July 19, 1973.

Other topics covered in my articles were the nesting habits of black skimmers, the reintroduction of the brown pelican, and the hatching of babies by Josephine — the mother lightning whelk — in the museum's saltwater aquarium.

On April 22, 1987, the lightning whelk became the Texas state shell. Curator Mildred Tate and museum President Jim McIver were the driving forces behind the effort to designate a state shell.

According to Jean Andrews in *Sea Shells of the Texas Gulf Coast*, the museum hosts the best shell collection along the Texas coast. Today the museum is housed in the Brazosport Center for the Arts and Sciences near Brazosport College.

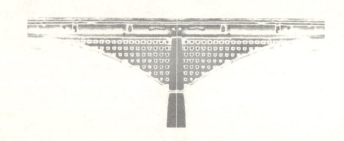

Family Spondylidea

Jagged, curved spines radiate
a fan pattern defining
chrysanthemum shells
living in the depths of the gulf
beyond the Texas coast.
Shells in bloom
secure in sharpness
establish territory
search for nourishment
search for mates
while embellishing
the Flower Garden Reef
like an interior designer
decorates a showroom vignette
in shades of white and cream
adding accents
of orange, yellow, or rose.
Like white and cream
chrysanthemums
accented
with orange, yellow, and rose
blooming
in the fall garden
establishing territory
absorbing life from the earth
absorbing life from the sun.
Like a poet lives a poem.

jelli 7

Sun streams weave through the ravine
shape leaves into a curtain of lace
a pulsating mandala
of shadow and silhouette.
A cardinal chirps out of sight
unconsciously changes
the design in the center of the circle.

Falling Star

I
In the dark of desert
a child questions her mother.
Did you fashion Falling Star?
No, mother replies then explains.
Grandmother Taos snipped
a feather from the comet's tail
and sent it fluttering to earth.

II
Somewhere along the third coast,
the astronomer-poet
tracks celestial intruders in the backyard.
He steps out of focus, rubs his eyes,
and watches Falling Star
streak across the sky
then weaves the glowing plumage
into a new poem.

III
Hale-Bopp, comet of some pomp,
comet of some circumstance,
observes his Lady walking on the beach.
In Prospero fashion he commands
his minion, Falling Star, to attract her.
Like Ariel, Falling Star blazes
to complete this romantic task.
His seine of stardust snares the Lady
whose wide eyes and warmed heart
bow to the comet and his fiery commotion.
Failing to realize demise comes on completion,
failing to remember Ariel flew to freedom,
Falling Star quietly slips below the horizon
forever quenched.

jelli 8

Moon
your illumination
is exquisite
in the backdrop
of night

you create
night exquisite
on the edge
of love field

Moon
your illumination
is exquisite
in the backdrop
of night
you create
night exquisite
on the edge
of love field
moon

The Night the Moon Fell

There was no thunder, quake, or tremor.
Even so, she floated in a puddle
of heart-shaped leaves under the redbud tree.

Set me back in the sky,
she implored with her eyes
as she struggled in the sea of hearts.

Her desperation demanded action.
My hands reached to her edges.
She slipped away.

I waited until the waves subsided
to snare the prize
but the hearts pushed me away.

Many times I reached
to free the moon from the trap of hearts.
Success eluded me.

With futility, I shook my head.
With grace, she dismissed me.
Closed her eyes.

Ponderings

Water sprites divide and multiply.
Spatter. Splash.
Sparkle.
Pose on the rocks
before drizzling down
to reflection and beyond.

Depth. Deep, deeper.
Color. Blue gray green black.
Temperature. Summer rewards
frogs and goldfish.
Winter isolates leaves
in ice jackets.

Reflection.
On one side birches green and white and healthy.
On the other dark Escheresque silhouettes.
Then a blade of grass and red begonia *pas de deux*
while crisp, brown leaves float aimlessly.
No ice insight.

Under reflection.
Goldfish swish dart grab and gobble.
Algae.
Who knows.
Does the pond have a basement.
Do the goldfish care.

Under under reflection.
Polyurethane.
Dirt rock brine oil steam
super-heated lava.
Core.
Ending. Beginning.

The Dance of the Brown Pelicans

man-stacked rocks
anchored with mexican moss
create a miniature maginot line
to repel the gulf of mexico
at san luis pass

placid waves
question the wall
sweet weather
forgets
storms of autumn
grind ships and shells
and solid investments
into a clay
of sand and fool's gold

everyday
rhythms of wind and moon advance
the edge of the gulf through the passage
into christmas bay
to taste the tidelands of chocolate bayou

once satiated the currents wild and free
tilt high tide back to the gulf
low tide follows in its wake

today
brown pelicans
whirl
their ritual of spirals
above the rocks
the waves and shifting sand

Moon Climb

December twilight fades
in the huge orange fullness.
Moon hides in clouds.
Now out.
Bleaching the tower.
Sparkling the granite capitol.
Floating in Town Lake.
Slipping past oak limbs
in the back canyon.

Stronger now
she watches Venus
gird the horizon
in magentas and lavenders.
Pause.
Stuck in a web of sticks.
Out.
Brighter.
Climbing.
Jupiter and Mars
marking the trail.

Pale and shimmering
she clings to a branch
high in the juniper.
Rests in thin air.
Prepares for the steep ascent
to midnight, eclipse, and beyond.

Reconciliation

Watermarked
sea green leaves
fan into a flat rosette
establishing itself to the edge
of the compost heap.
Eventually entwining tangles
gild the pungent leaves
with gaudy yellow flowers
while vines glide across the path
in a prodigal return
to the garden
presenting gifts
of butternut squash
along the way.

Leaf Dreams

I
In spring pale golden hearts
unfurl wrinkled and damp
after the redbud
drizzles the garden pink.
In summer heart-shaped favorites
sing green harmonies.
In fall burnished hearts
bright and brittle
unravel their moorings.

In between
spent lacy hearts
flutter to the ground.

In winter
fragile hearts shatter underfoot;
tears soften the edges.

II
A brass cast rutabaga leaf.
Edges crimped. Gold veined.
Patterned memory of another.

III
The leaf in eddy
floats beneath the bridge.
It rides and rolls in swift swirls,
trembles on the edge of the whirlpool.

Trembles in. Slides out.
Disappears in rapids to drown.
Or survives if a young girl
rescues, dries, and counts it
as her treasure.

I never saw the leaf.
The poet sketched the words of leaves.
His watermarks and stains
share empathy.

IV
Fast water.
High water.
Shallow water.
Undertow.
Whirlpools
spin me and other leaves
down to cold dark regions
whirl us up to warm springs.

Then I remember
from time to time
the slow flooding river spreads
across the swamp
to my back door.
Once,
the hurricane tidal surge swept
through our house —
took for its own my young girl's treasure.

Lady of the Yucatan

Uri Caynne
goddess of myth and fantasy
mother of the Urricans of high summer
plays siren to porpoise
as they romp relentlessly
in the undulating gulf.

Her long laboring swells
shove past jetties
contracting galaxies
into spiraling hurricanes
into delicate shells.

She refurbishes fertility,
distills the rain,
refills the rivers —
sometimes to overflowing
under the seasons of the moon.

Tiring of porpoise teasing
she sanctifies the saltwater
as raw energy surges in her heart,
breaking over barrier islands
in waves of creativity.

Demise of Names

Weathermen once assigned
feminine names and wiles
to hurricanes
and still do for that matter
as they follow
those defined eyes
shadowed in counter-clockwise makeup
as they track and stalk
with masculine determination.

Now, along the Gulf Coast
from Port Isabel to Freeport
from Galveston to Cameron
from Biloxi and Mobile Bay
few women answer to Audrey
Beulah
Alicia
Carla
Celia or
Camille.

In 2001
Houstonians
crossed
Allison
off the list.

jelli 9

flowing through fall branches
conduits of rain
spin strings of leaves to earth

flowing through
fall branches
conduits of rain
spin strings
of leaves to earth
flowing through
fall branches
conduits of rain
spin strings
of leaves to earth

Night Designs

Hear the honking song
the high away sound of spring
as it is now
as it was
when geese patterned flyways
above buffalo, passenger pigeons,
and rivers flowing clear. The geese
etched their silhouette in Vee
across the silver moon.

Hear the honking song
the high away sound of fall
as it was
as it is now.
Geese follow their flyways
beneath blinking satellites
mourning the pigeons and buffalo
watching muddy rivers
sour the landscape.
Then a Vee formation stretches a veil
over the moon's ravaged face.

jelli 10

reike flashed in circles
transcendent to you
then back to me
through leaves and limbs
and deep roots under the rose
touching me touching you

reike flashed in circles
transcendent to you
then back to me
through leaves and
limbs and deep roots
under the rose
touching me
touching you

touching me
touching you

Melody of Loons

the storm approaches
mother sits and watches and waits

the water ripples
circles expand
young loons hover overhead
then dive
soon fog covers the lake
in harmony with the loons

fall comes early in the north
loons fly east to the sea
where they winter in ocean swells
and prepare for spring's long journey

listen
look
the loons are back

the storm approaches
mother sits and waits

Electric Ice

A blue norther
sneaks past moon towers
in the capital city
ignoring the calendar
dragging drizzle and freezing rain
over old Waterloo
sticking sleet on bridges
coating fall in straitjackets
clear and icy.

Ice prisoners
crash across power lines
transforming night to day
in shock waves of Aurora
in magenta and turquoise flashes
exploding transformers
above canyons and creeks.

Then gas-fired logs gleam
in the fireplace
replacing the glow of computer
while electric ice
decorates parts of the city
as hot icicles hang
eave on eave
over tree and shrub
and flowerpot
ignoring have-nots shivering
in the dark.

Whitecaps and Ravens

The cold east wind and churning gulf crash
on the jetties
on the beach
on themselves.

Ancient waves and wind
wrap my solitude in a scarf
unraveling its edges.
I walk the still damp path
with eyes down and searching.
Ocean gods neglect me.
No Sand Dollars, Olives, or Shark's Eyes.
No birds brave the gale.
Finally, the ocean remembers.
A shiny Olive and a small Sand Dollar
appear in the newest wind row.
A thank you issues from my heart
and squawking invades my ears.
My eyes meet a rare beach distraction.
Perched high in the roots of a once-proud oak,
two ravens invade my reverie.

A seam of time opens.

I watch my parents
preen elegant feathers.
Conversation surrounds me.
>	Earl: *"I knew she wouldn't notice us."*
>	Violet: *"Shhh. You'll disturb her search."*

The seam of time closes.

Storm Wobbles

Replacing horsetails of yesterday,
the valley-ripened, ruby red sun clabbers
buttermilk skies over the pink granite capitol
while a tropical storm wobbles
east southeast of Freeport in the Gulf of Mexico.
Now, rain bands sweep across scars
in hill country quarries ravaged over time
to build a capitol to anchor the state,
forced to sacrifice birthrights from ancient seas
to forge a jetty and save the mouth of the Brazos.

Rain and time wobble back
to the almost deserted jetty
where Violet views porpoise gliding upstream
and algae-stained swells spawn salty geysers
drenching the foolhardy stalking the elusive redfish.
Nearby, in the Intracoastal Waterway
shrimp boats parade one behind another
forcing the pontoon bridge to swing open
as the fleet runs for river refuge
in the tree-lined San Bernard.

Outside the National Bank of Freeport,
a clerk unlocks the glass showcase,
tacks up a teletype advisory.
Gale force winds by nightfall.
After checking the news under glass,
Violet steams a storm-watch jambalaya
with commentary for dessert.
When horsetails fly overhead
and porpoise play upriver
watch for a storm in the gulf.
Be wary when buttermilk clabbers the sky
and the sun rises red in the morning.

Dream Flares and Thunder Drops

Anvils in clouds rack the evening sky
flaring into thunder drops
pounding the salt grass prairie.
A net-covered lapis sphere
cools Violet's hand. As North Pole snuggles
against her palm, South struggles against her thumb.
Quaking continents rearrange the surface
revealing a gateway to Edinburgh.

Tracing the gate, she leaps like Alice
landing on the balcony of birds.
Time bends over the coffee table
as Minotaur smashes the drizzling mimosas
and awakes Swan atop the bookcase
sheltering I. M. Pei, Philip Glass, and Gustav Klimt.

Sine waves undulate and propel Swan
beyond Orion and his operation
of confining Time into crystal bricks
where trees without leaves
sift shadows across the bedroom wall.

Violet slides beneath sheets and layers of ifs,
noting a difference in caress,
in intensity. She slips away in rain,
lightning, hail, and thunder
as dreams divide and multiply
creating a mandala layered
in shuttered windows,
clustered brass leaves, and Violet's shadow
surrounding marbles snared
in waves and nets.
Swans and twin flames flare the center.

from Conversations with Two Rivers

Terry Everett and I met in Taos, New Mexico, during a week long workshop directed by Nancy Wood. My fascination with *Spirit Walker* had provided the motivation to attend her poetry workshop offered by the Taos Institute of Art.

In *Spirit Walker's* preface, Nancy mentions dancing in hiking boots on mountaintops to the music of Vivaldi. She wears a long, flowing purple dress over parka and jeans as she dances on the Continental Divide. There, she pays homage to the mountains, renews herself, and becomes free.

I had to go to Taos to meet this woman who dances on mountaintops. I had to learn to dance on the mountains and so I did.

Our group began the days at the Taos Art Gallery Bed and Breakfast with lectures and discussions. In the afternoons our field trips took us to mountain meadows, the mesa above the Rio Grande gorge, the Taos ski valley, and the Taos Pueblo and cemetery where we cried.

The initial idea for "Relative Relativity" began to take shape when the group was provided the writing prompt, family circles.

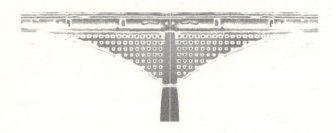

Relative Relativity

Family circles
overlap and expand
like drops on the lakes
of solar systems
in the Milky Way —
products of creation
with unlimited possibilities.
So many generations
we cannot see
to the edges.

Family circles
nurtured by sun,
moon, earth, and stars —
sometimes warm
and loving
sometimes cold
and feuding.
So many generations
we cannot see
to the edges.

from Conversations with Two Rivers

About the time Daddy was elected Grand Knight of the Lake Jackson Chapter of the Knights of Columbus, young Father Patrick came to St. Michael's to assist Monsignor Leo Wleczyk.

Daddy took Father Pat under his wing and taught him the fine details of parish life. Daddy had already trained Father Leo when Leo was a pitcher for Daddy's little league team, the Dodgers — one of the first little league teams in Freeport, Texas.

After Daddy died, it was with a bit of trepidation that I shared my poem, "Whitecaps and Ravens," (p. 89) with Father Pat. He listened intently as I recited the poem to him and then said, "So that's where he went."

I am sure I looked stunned at his comment, and Father Pat said, "Didn't you know that after Earl died a crow used to tease Thursday morning mass-goers as they left the church going to the parish hall for coffee?"

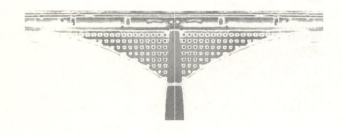

Raven Legion

April Fool's Day.
Daddy's choice
for leaving the earth realm
to join the Raven Legion.

No raven could comfort the daughter.
No raven could tell her not to cry.
No raven could comfort Father Patrick.
No raven could tell him not to cry.

That evening
Father Patrick consoled the daughter
saying you have lost a parent
and I have lost a friend.

At the funeral
Father Patrick cried.
Then ravens and people alike
knew great sadness.

Later on the beach
Earl cheered his daughter.
Greeted her squawking loudly
and flapping his wings. She smiled.

Sometime later at the church
Earl cheered Father Patrick
and the Thursday morning faithful
with loud squawking and flapping of wings.

Section Five:

5

from the depths of ancient coolers

from Conversations with Two Rivers

In July 1996, I attended a weekend workshop titled "Rebirth and Dreams of the Soul" at the Jung Center in Houston, Texas. I still have the clay chalice I created in Irene Corbit's art workshop while we listened to myths and fairy tales in the darkened studio. I also participated in Dr. Roger Woolger's active imagination seminar. During his session, I imagined myself at Mont-Saint-Michel during the start of the Children's Crusade. Then, I danced to the guided meditation, "Temple by the Sea," under Carolyn Fay's direction as part of her expressive arts program.

Two months later, in Taos, New Mexico, while some members of Nancy Wood's writing workshop climbed a mountain trail in the Ski Valley, I sat beside a mountain stream and "Ritual in Clay" began to flow across my journal page.

Later in October my poem, "Acequias in Shadow," (p. 49) was born. On that last day when I should have been packing, Taos Mountain forced me to sit and watch her ceremony of shadows across the valley.

"Acequias in Shadow" also links back to my first class in Taos at Dr. John Muste's home where we studied the Water Politics of Northern New Mexico.

Acequia is the Spanish word for ditch and came to the language through the Moorish influence. We studied Stanley Crawford's *Mayordomo* and *The Garlic Testament* and John Nichols' *The Milagro Beanfield War*. We had firsthand experience of the *acequia* system as we visited the Crawford garlic farm.

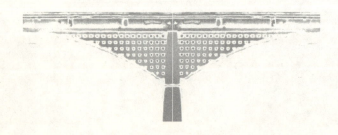

Ritual in Clay

Above the Sangre de Cristos
mist matures to rain
while soft, cold essentials
surround the poet
trickling down her face
creating slender streams along the trail
rushing through the Rio Grande gorge
weaving to the coastal plains
seeking reunion with the warm gulf waters.

As rain continues soft and cold
rain candles flare at eventide
searing a seam in time. She shivers.
Steps beyond the porch,
nods to the mountain, lifts the clay chalice
to catch the life sustaining drops
the fluid of ancient odysseys.
She sips mulled wine
soothing the seam.

Fragrance of rain
hovers in the candle glow
while fiery tongues and raindrops
form slender streams
flowing soft and cold
across the windowpane
carving out canyons
rushing to the coast
floating to the ancestral home.

jelli 11

then
watch the leonids and perseids
fall across the predawn sky
watch the stars
burn across the galaxy

then
dream a poem

then watch the
leonids and perseids
fall across the
predawn sky watch
the stars burn
across the galaxy
then dream a poem

then
dream

The Style of Two Rivers

As she considers
and reconsiders
the creative act
of writing a poem,
she believes
personal freedom
is paramount.

As the pen travels across
the page freely as a brush
caressing a canvas —
anything can happen.

Suddenly, without
forethought or plan,
freedom and the unknown
must and do appear.

The final process,
the final position of words
is destined to become
the product of regeneration
past memories relit
and gelled under present light
into a new creation.

Waiting for Poetry

I wait in dim emptiness
for poetry hiding backstage
behind the proscenium arch,
behind the pleats of tormentors and teasers.

The exposed set glares.
Its simplicity scratches imagination.
Ignites a memory of *Our Town*.
The stage right stepladder points
upward to the warmth of the gelled spotlight
flooding the podium downstage.

I wait. The podium waits.
Waits for the poet, the stage manager, or both.
Soon, masters of poetry and podium meet
beside the ladder in the circle of light.

There, poet and poetry unwind
streamers of satin and grosgrain ribbon
into words and rhythms
floating downstage
fusing the air I hear.
The air I breathe.
I inhale.
Poetry sighs. Poetry sings.

Spumoni Ink

Recalling some Shakespeare.
Remembering Chaucer.
Considering signs of spring.

In letters larger than life
Talisman traces itself on the hill
beyond lavender wisteria vines
twisting with writhing arms
and legs conjuring the hint
of mystique and charms
waiting in cliff-hugging flats.

Under Romeo's café sign
of hearts and flying angels,
spring sneezes and ruffles roses
climbing over long suffering swans.
Gasoline gulping weedeaters,
spewing Puck-like noise and vexation,
out-buzz bees while very public kisses
flavor the heart-healthy pasta primavera.

Showers sweep April across the piazza
as the spumoni melts into ink
meandering into pistachio words
etching cherry-almond impressions
of lovers lost in the margin.

from Conversations with Two Rivers

It was mid-December in Taos, New Mexico, and Natalie Goldberg was conducting her workshop on writing, creativity, and meditation in the studio of the Mable Dodge Luhan House.

I wore patent leather boots to walk across the snow-covered parking lot to the studio. During our meditation, our sitting moments, I wondered about snow...

I had seen snow about four times in Brazosport, Texas, and about two times in Austin, Texas. I saw snow in the Rockies and the Alps in the summer but I didn't walk in it.

Once, I traveled to New York on a drama tour with Dr. Robert G. Everding. It was just after I finished my master's degree at the University of Houston/Clear Lake and between semesters at UH/CL. Christmas decorations were still up in January, and it was deep-freeze cold with snow flurries. New Yorkers were not pleased.

I wore suede boots and enjoyed myself as we stood in line at Times Square and purchased tickets for Amadeus, PT Barnum, Crimes of the Heart, and The Dresser...

My shiny boots must have amused Ms. Goldberg, and she mentioned them when she autographed my copy of her book, Living Color.

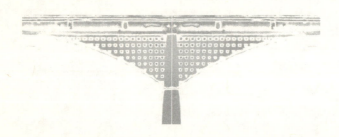

Bell Power

Church bells echo and fade
across the Rio Grande,
snug in the shadows of the gorge
ever widening, splitting the mesa.
Then Natalie strikes her bowl bell.
Conversation halts.
Sitting moments commence.

Stunning resonance widens eyes —
eases into ears
hums past lips
rolls over tongues
slips into the skin —
energizing the body.
Vibrations weave a double helix
tuning the collective soul.

Taos Mountain nods in reply,
etched in the many-paned window
framing imagination.

Writing practice
folds words
simple and exquisite
into everyday stories.
Shared reading
transforms scribbles
into tales universal
floating over lips
circling the room
slipping out the window
flying over the mountain
churning down the gorge.

jelli 12

As the censer swings
red moon pales into blue nights
sailing through memory
longing for the rain
wishing for the dance.
In the sanctuary of imagination.

As the censer swings
red moon pales
into blue nights
sailing through
memory **longing**
for the rain
wishing for **the dance.**
In the sanctuary
of **imagination**

First Fountain

Splashes, dribbles, and drips.

Creative rhythms
wrinkle the pool
supersaturate the air
conceal its source
impede my search.

Drops cling to hair.
She slips and stumbles on the path.

Splashes, dribbles, and drips
fill sensory avenues
to overflowing
louder and louder
as the veil of concealment
turns transparent.

Anticipation vibrates anticipation.

She stumbles.
Slips.
Staggers forward
to the emerging fountain
inside its circle of marble.

Slender spikes of water protect
the central geyser of liquid motion.
Suddenly — spikes collapse.

A solitary column relaxes
in a double helix
crumbling to the turbulence
calming into quiet.

Metamorphosis

a wish for freedom
to fly above the norm
a wish for elegance
to delight

the wishes
drown in a mix
of vanilla coffee and kahlua
while the phonograph needle
hangs in the final groove
silencing the Tiajuana Brass

Tree Trance

I sink
with ease
through mattress
and floor
into the earth
to rest in a cradle
of roots and limestone
receiving energy
releasing tangles.

I dream
a tree trance moment
with left foot and ankle
across my right calf
left arm draping
my breast.
Auras spark
stones and roots
trunks and branches
challenging Aurora.
Bells clang
along the escarpment.

On the Way to Poetry

Red and white and silver.
One aluminum can
rolls and bounces
along the pavement
of the two-lane country road,

in harm's way and out,

riding the waves of wind
across the prairie road
unfolding FM 102
in a straight, flat-line contrast
with the hilly road
left behind
curving from Columbus.

A straight line
beside the straight-line railroad track
beside the rattling rattlesnake
cuts through the gulf prairie
to Eagle Lake and beyond.

The blue heron sits
watching
beside the pond
day by day
sits everyday beside
his own private pond lined
with cattails and dragonflies
on the edge of Eagle Lake.
Sits there in his
blueness
alone like a poet,

on the edge
of experimental fields
of blue corn and red bluebonnets.

In other fields along Eagle Lake
white birds ride furrows
searching for grasshoppers
behind the tractor
like sea gulls
skimming waves
snatching mullet
in the wake of trolling nets
and shrimp boats.

Gulls and egrets
create a cloud
above Eagle Lake
and the white donkey
waits patiently in the shade
beside the sulphur spill
that still yellows the ground
that poisons the earth
in years beyond memory.
Nearby
a rainbow of laundry
hangs on a fence
as it did the other day.

Nearer the gulf —
on the Pledger road —
trees broken
and twisted by the storm
stand beside the roof of a barn
ripped by the wind.
The top of the porch
reclines across the front door
of the house
because the poet
in the storm
swirled and spun
and twisted
the air under the cover of the rain.

jelli 13

on the edge of love field
cool drowsy mornings
linger on the page
creole evenings
boil the ink
melt the pen

on the edge
of love field
cool drowsy mornings
linger on the page
creole evenings
boil the ink
melt the pen

creole
evenings

Afternoon of Gulls

Sculptured feathers
color-blocked stripes
litter the path
like Easter eggs
in Grandma's backyard
like sand dollars
on San Luis beach.

In beachcomber rhythm
I collect quills and speculate
will they spread ink across a page
will the ink seep into words.

Then ...
carnage blocks the way.
A dead gull floats in a pool
of blood. Neck bent. Head hiding
under the remaining outstretched wing.

Overhead
gulls dive and whirl a requiem
snatching soggy fries
        from a red- and yellow-striped vessel
                offering comic relief
evading questions.

jelli 14

poet
of water, sand, and salt
already old
when ancient Sanskrit
was young
translate me
with your pen and ink
in pure and private context

poet of water,
sand, and salt
already old when
ancient Sanskrit was
young translate me
with your pen and ink
in pure and private
context

poet
of water

Lines and Waves

High tide on Bryan Beach
entangles a lightning whelk
a chipped wine glass
a monarch butterfly
in fragments
of net and seaweed.
Low tide
strands the tangle
in a wind row
strangely out of element.

Strangely out of element
she floats in the lyric sounds of the sea
in the sea sounds of the poet.
Tidal lyrics
crash on sandbars
gasp in breakers
struggle for words
smearing the ink.

jelli 15

Sine and cosine bewilder
with opposite over hypotenuse
adjacent over hypotenuse.
While mentor recites
the Pythagorean theorem,
poet considers
the transmigration of the soul.

Sine and cosine
bewilder with opposite
over hypotenuse
adjacent over
hypotenuse.
While mentor recites
the Pythagorean
theorem, poet
considers the
transmigration of the
soul

Two Rivers' Song

Twin flames.
Our spirits touched
in the cosmic long ago.
We loved before we were.
I was. You were.
Brother Sister Mother Father
Mentor Student Wife Husband
Sweetheart Lover Life.

In different realms,
your creative genius
sparks my creativity.
A single arc across a universe
as Aurora regenerates
illuminations across galaxies.

Design and symbol
delineate poetry drama and music
in spatial harmony.

Time travel
comes without tethers or chains
to spirits soaring
on waves above waves
from uncharted shores
to inmind seas.

This moment of lost illusion
finds you swimming crosscurrent
battling the undertow of indecision
flood tides of doubt.
Do not fear the fire and ice
of healing and renewal.
Lights of illusion expand
with starbursts of inspiration.

Interview with the Author

#1 — *Someone once said, to be a recognized poet one must write about political issues. What current issues do you write about?*

    I write about coastal and city issues of environment, industrial growth, offshore and onshore oil drilling, urban sprawl, roads and streets, drainage and flood control, education, defense and space exploration. These issues revolve around conversations with family and friends and even strangers I meet on the train. The conversations then squirm around in my journal notes and often emerge in poems such as "Sleeping Arrangements #41," "Tugs and Barges," and "The Dance of the Brown Pelicans."

#2 — *What are your earliest, artistic memories that link to your writing craft?*

    St. Mary-Star of the Sea, a small Catholic church in Freeport, Texas, was the site of my first sense of drama. There, the precision of Mass at center stage flourished in high feast day celebrations with color, light, symbolic vestments, responsive readings, and classical music. This experience came before I started school, and I thought I was attending a play when I went to Mass with my parents.

    I feel I was born with a sense of what looks right or wrong in a stage picture. With that skill in place, my mentors from Little Theatre of Brazosport and my graduate school professor, Dr. Robert G. Everding, taught me to fine tune a play presented on the arena stage.

    As both stage manager and director, I learned to view and direct a dramatic scene from all four sides and angles of the arena. With the addition of my early childhood memory of responsive reading, color, light, symbolism, and music, my sense of fine tuning a poem was born during my early theatrical training. I just didn't know it at the time.

#3 — *What was your original poetic inspiration?*

    My poetic inspiration starts with memories of family laced with the coastal landscape of Brazoria County, home to parts of my family for six generations.

    Much later, a different type of inspiration came to me from Natalie Goldberg. During a workshop in Taos, New Mexico, she taught that improvement in writing comes as a writer pursues a second creative endeavor. In my case, drama was my creative focus long before I ever considered writing poetry. I once created realism and fantasy and all that flows between on stage. Now, from my dramatic foundation, I weave energy and symbolism of words into my poetry.

#4 — *When did you start to write poetry?*
My poetry adventure began in the 1990s as I participated in the four-year bible study course, Education for Ministry, at St. Timothy's Episcopal Church in Lake Jackson, Texas. The popular course reflects the core curriculum of the University of the South, and my classmates were exposed to some of my earliest poetic attempts.

#5 — *Do you need to hear the roar of the gulf or a mountain stream as you compose your poetry?*
Most of my tideland poetry has been composed since I moved to Austin. Maybe I needed the long view of the coast that comes to me in these Austin hills in order to formulate my coastal images.

My driest poems started before we moved to Austin when I went to writing workshops in New Mexico. "Across the Rio Grande Rift" and "Vacation in Taos" reflect memories of shadows in the Sangre de Cristos mountains. My walking-on-the-beach poem, "Erased," published in *3 Savanna Blue*, was born during a Taos writing exercise.

#6 — *Do you have a writing support group?*
John Reding, my husband, is the business manager for my writing adventures. Theresa Reding, Regina Zeyzus, and John proofread the galleys for *Antonelli's River Inn* and *3 Savanna Blue*.

My self-proclaimed writing partner is Glynn Irby. Our original artistic relationship started in the 1970s when I was directing arena stage productions at the Little Theatre of Brazosport. Glynn designed the sets for two of my shows, *The Girls in 509* and *The Unexpected Guest*, my Master of Arts project at the University of Houston/Clear Lake.

We began sharing our poetry in the fall of 1994. First, we shared poetic rough drafts. Then, we developed a gentle push/pull critique method that struggles through abstract concepts and searches for succinct expression while we consider rhythm and the visual image of the poem on the page. Gentle as it is, the push/pull process often lasts for weeks or more as we hone a poem to its completion through e-mail and telephone conversations.

#7 — *What is the goal of poetry and what is its single benefit to you?*

Poetry's single benefit to me is the freedom to compress everything from early childhood memories to the changing scene outside my studio into word monuments of my life experience.

The goal of poetry is to preserve the human experience for future generations, and the sport of preservation is accessible to all. We are born with imagination and everything necessary for a would-be writer to activate his or her imagination. To ignite this writing process, the writer needs only to push a pencil across recycled paper.

#8 — *Why are some of your poems titled "jelli" plus a number?*

The jellies are from my collection of untitled poems. They are called jellies because, like jelly beans, they can be sweet, sour, hot, spicy, full of color, or black and white. The numbers give them an identity.

#9 — *Why did you decide to have "from Conversations with Two Rivers" introduce some of your poems?*

First, I watched and listened to Robert Bly perform and read his poetry in Austin, Texas. As well, I observed Coleman Banks reading his poetry in Houston, Texas. Both poets often introduced their work in a casual, conversational style.

So, I decided to implement a similar style of introduction in my readings. Once I implemented this approach, I began to notice the audiences' reactions. Eyes lit up with appreciation. Folks nodded approval and sometimes they grinned and smiled. Afterwards, they said they liked the extra remarks.

Secondly, when I studied in Taos, New Mexico, my mentors, Nancy Wood, Natalie Goldberg, Jimmy Santiago Baca, and John Nichols presented introductory remarks that enhanced the reading of their work.

I have just followed the example of some of the best contemporary poets and writers.

10 — *Why did you dedicate your poem, "Saturday Morning at Sainte-Mere-Eglise," to Dr. Stephen Ambrose and Senator George McGovern?*

I met both men in Innsbruck, Austria, as part of the summer school program sponsored by the University of New Orleans on the campus of Innsbruck University. I met Dr. Ambrose first in the summer of 1984.

I heard Dr. Ambrose deliver the orientation address at the start of the summer program. The address was impressive, and I decided to enroll in one of his classes at the first opportunity.

My chance came in 1987 when Dr. Ambrose taught the history of World War II in the European Theatre. We took a weekend trip to visit the Normandy invasion area. There we visited the site of the short but strategic battle of Pegasus Bridge, which is the main topic of Ambrose's book by the same name.

In the shadow of the bridge, Dr. Ambrose introduced us to World War II veterans: Maj. John Howard from England and Col. Hans A. von Luck from Germany — both players in the war drama.

Major Howard commanded glider troops that crash landed near the bridge and secured it in the early morning hours of D-Day. A regiment of Panzers in the nearby area of Caen was commanded by Col. von Luck. He waited for orders that never came.

The field trip was stunning. As an American history teacher, I was fortunate to visit D-Day sites of such historic magnitude and to be in the company of these courageous men.

I met Senator George McGovern, a veteran pilot of World War II, in the summer of 1985 and took his course, "The Diplomatic History of the United States from 1945." Our textbook was titled, *Rise to Globalism*, by Dr. Ambrose.

Both men were the featured presenters of the Wednesday Night Forum during the summers I was in Innsbruck. After the forum, we adjourned to the Innrain Café where we casually continued the forum topics. Often I sat at the same table with Senator McGovern or Dr. Ambrose.

I was privileged to share in the conversations and lectures of these two distinguished gentlemen.

Biographies

Carlyn Luke Reding, a sixth generation Texan, is a Brazoria County native and lives in Austin, Texas. She earned degrees at the University of Houston/Clear Lake and the University of Texas. She taught English and social studies in the Brazosport Public Schools.

Her poetry is published in *New Texas 2002, Texas Poetry Calendar 2003, Suddenly V, Along Life's Paths, Red Boots & Attitude, 3 Savanna Blue, Houston Poetry Fest 99, Feeding the Crow,* and *DiVerseCity* anthologies. Periodicals, newspapers, and e-zines in which her poetry has been featured include the *Austin Writer, Image Magazine* of Brazoria County, the *Brazosport Facts, Stazja's Map,* and *Sol Magazine.*

Reding has been a poetry judge for the Young Texas Writers at the Writers' League of Texas, the Brazosport Poets' Society, and the Southern Literary Festival 2000 at The University of Louisiana at Monroe.

She belongs to the Writers' League of Texas, the Austin International Poetry Festival, Poetry in the Arts, and the Houston International Poets. She supports the Texas Exes and the Little Theatre of Brazosport as a lifetime member and reads poetry with the Galveston Poets' Roundtable.

Reding is also a storyteller and teaches creativity and writing workshops in secondary schools, colleges, and universities.

Glynn Monroe Irby holds a B.A. in history from the University of Texas at Austin. He also has completed studies in the field of history at the University of Houston, Brazosport College, and Edinburgh University in Scotland. Additional educational studies include graduate work in architecture at the University of Houston.

Irby has served as graphic designer for the Austin International Poetry Fest anthology and Houston International Poetry anthology. He has also worked as the graphic designer on two poetry books: *3 Savanna Blue* by Irby, Reding, and Peggy

Zuleika Lynch, and *Silhouette to Unheard Music* by Lynch.

Irby is a member of the Writers' League of Texas and the Galveston Poets' Roundtable. He is a professional member of the American Society of Interior Designers. Currently, Irby manages a long-standing family furniture and design business in Brazoria County, Texas.

Susie Kelly Flatau is an author, editor, speaker and workshop presenter. Between 1996 and 2003, she has authored and co-authored four books: *Red Boots & Attitude, From My Mother's Hands, Counter Culture Texas,* and *Reaching Out to Today's Kids.* Her short fiction has also appeared in *New Texas 2000.* She has written for various newspapers and magazines — *Austin American-Statesman, Good Life, Gusto, Women's Monthly, Enchanted Rock,* and *South Texas Traveler.* She has also written a script for *Earth and Sky radio.*

Flatau's speaking engagements, book talks, and workshops on writing memoirs and life stories have resulted in international (Germany, upon invitation by the U.S. Army for Women's History Month), national, and regional travels.

Flatau's professional affiliations include the Writers' League of Texas, National Association of Women Writers, Women Writing the West, Texas Oral History Association, Texas Folklore Society, and Story Circle Network. She lives in Austin, Texas, with her husband Jack.